HISTORIC CIVILIZATIONS

ANCIENT MESOPOTAMIA

John Malam

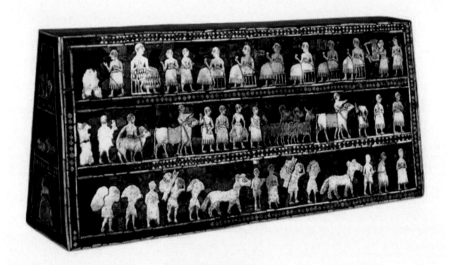

GARETH**STEVENS**
GS
PUBLISHING
A World Almanac Education Group Company

How to use this book

Each topic in this book is clearly labeled and contains all these components:

Topic heading ———

Introduction to the topic ———

Words that are in the topic glossary are bolded the first time they appear on the page. ———

Subtopic 1 gives information about one aspect of the topic. ———

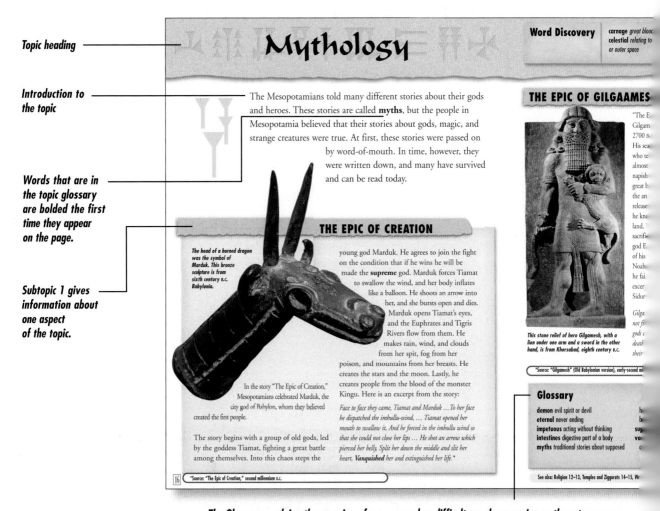

Mythology

Word Discovery   carnage *great bloo[d]*
celestial *relating to or outer space*

The Mesopotamians told many different stories about their gods and heroes. These stories are called **myths**, but the people in Mesopotamia believed that their stories about gods, magic, and strange creatures were true. At first, these stories were passed on by word-of-mouth. In time, however, they were written down, and many have survived and can be read today.

THE EPIC OF CREATION

The head of a horned dragon was the symbol of Marduk. This bronze sculpture is from sixth century B.C. Babylonia.

In the story "The Epic of Creation," Mesopotamians celebrated Marduk, the city god of Babylon, whom they believed created the first people.

The story begins with a group of old gods, led by the goddess Tiamat, fighting a great battle among themselves. Into this chaos steps the young god Marduk. He agrees to join the fight on the condition that if he wins he will be made the **supreme** god. Marduk forces Tiamat to swallow the wind, and her body inflates like a balloon. He shoots an arrow into her, and she bursts open and dies. Marduk opens Tiamat's eyes, and the Euphrates and Tigris Rivers flow from them. He makes rain, wind, and clouds from her spit, fog from her poison, and mountains from her breasts. He creates the stars and the moon. Lastly, he creates people from the blood of the monster Kingu. Here is an excerpt from the story:

Face to face they came, Tiamat and Marduk ... To her face he dispatched the imhullu-wind, .., Tiamat opened her mouth to swallow it, And he forced in the imhullu wind so that she could not close her lips ... He shot an arrow which pierced her belly, Split her down the middle and slit her heart, Vanquished her and extinguished her life.*

16   *Source: "The Epic of Creation," second millennium B.C.*

THE EPIC OF GILGAAMES[H]

"The E[pic of] Gilgam[esh] 2700 B[.C.] His sea[rch] who te[lls] almost napish[tim] great h[e] the an[...] release[...] he kne[w] land. [...] sacrifi[ce] god E[...] of his [...] Noah[...] he fai[...] excer[pt] Sidur[...]

Gilga[...] not fi[...] gods t[...] death[...] their [...]

This stone relief of hero Gilgamesh, with a lion under one arm and a sword in the other hand, is from Khorsabad, eighth century B.C.

Source: "Gilgamesh" (Old Babylonian version), early-second mi[...]

Glossary

demon evil spirit or devil
eternal never ending
impetuous acting without thinking
intestines digestive part of a body
myths traditional stories about supposed

See also: Religion 12–13, Temples and Ziggurats 14–15, Wr[...]

The Glossary explains the meaning of any unusual or difficult words appearing on these two pages.

Please visit our web site at: **www.garethstevens.com**
For a free color catalog describing Gareth Stevens Publishing's list of high-quality books and multimedia programs, call 1-800-542-2595 (USA) or 1-800-387-3178 (Canada). Gareth Stevens Publishing's fax: (414) 332-3567.

Library of Congress Cataloging-in-Publication Data

Malam, John, 1957-
  Ancient Mesopotamia / by John Malam.
    p. cm. — (Historic civilizations)
  Includes index.
  ISBN 0-8368-4199-9 (lib. bdg.)
  1. Iraq—Civilization—To 634—Juvenile literature. I. Title. II. Series.
DS71.M35   2004
935—dc22   2004045303

This North American edition first published in 2005 by
Gareth Stevens Publishing
A World Almanac Education Group Company
330 West Olive Street, Suite 100
Milwaukee, Wisconsin 53212 USA

This U.S. edition copyright © 2005 by Gareth Stevens, Inc. Original edition copyright © 2004 ticktock Entertainment Ltd. First published in Great Britain in 2004 as *Your Mesopotamia (Ancient Iraq) Homework Helper* by ticktock Media Ltd., Unit 2, Orchard Business Centre, North Farm Road, Tunbridge Wells, Kent TN23XF, UK.

The publishers wish to thank Roger Matthews, Michael Seymour, Institute of Archaeology at University College London, and Egan-Reid Ltd. for their research and consulting expertise in the making of this book.

Gareth Stevens editor: Barbara Kiely Miller
Gareth Stevens cover design: Steve Schraenkler

Printed in the United States of America

1 2 3 4 5 6 7 8 9 08 07 06 05 04

Contents

Subtopic 2 gives information about another aspect of the topic.

Discover other words that relate to the topic.

The Case Study is a closer look at a famous person, artifact, or building that relates to the topic.

epic *long poem about hero; art or events of great length*
grotesque *ugly*

immortality *living forever*
moral *related to principles of right and wrong behavior*

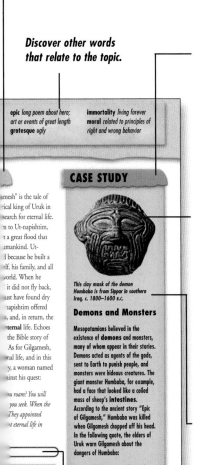

CASE STUDY

...amesh" is the tale of ...rical king of Uruk in ...search for eternal life. ...n to Ut-napishtim, ...t a great flood that ...mankind. Ut-...l because he built a ...lf, his family, and all ...world. When he ...it did not fly back, ...ust have found dry ...napishtim offered ..., and, in return, the ...ternal life. Echoes ...the Bible story of ...As for Gilgamesh, ...nal life, and in this ...y, a woman named ...ainst his quest:

...u roam? You will ...you seek. When the ...They appointed ...t eternal life in

This clay mask of the demon Humbaba is from Sippar in southern Iraq, c. 1800–1600 B.C.

Demons and Monsters

Mesopotamians believed in the existence of **demons** and monsters, many of whom appear in their stories. Demons acted as agents of the gods, sent to Earth to punish people, and monsters were hideous creatures. The giant monster Humbaba, for example, had a face that looked like a coiled mass of sheep's **intestines.** According to the ancient story "Epic of Gilgamesh," Humbaba was killed when Gilgamesh chopped off his head. In the following quote, the elders of Uruk warn Gilgamesh about the dangers of Humbaba:

*You are (still young), Gilgamesh, you are **impetuous** ... But you do not know what you will find ... Humbaba, whose shout is the flood weapon, Whose utterance is fire and whose breath is death, Can hear for up to sixty leagues the sound of his forest.**

Each photo or illustration is described and discussed in the accompanying text.

Captions clearly explain what is in the picture.

*Source: "Gilgamesh" (Standard version), early-first millennium B.C.

At the bottom of some sections, a reference bar tells where the information has come from.

...ry to explain ...e natural world ...or quality ...n a battle or

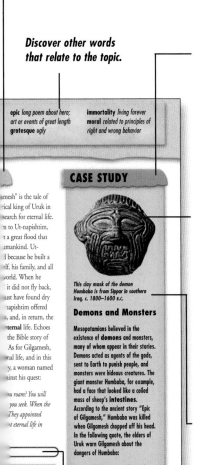
day Life 28–29

Other pages in the book that relate to what you have read in this topic are listed here.

A reference bar marked with an asterisk (*) gives the source of the quotations in the text.

Mesopotamia	4
Nomads to City Dwellers	6
The People	8
Palaces and Houses	10
Religion	12
Temples and Ziggurats	14
Mythology	16
Writing and Law	18
Wars and Weapons	20
Farming and Food	22
Arts and Craft	24
Science and Medicine	26
Everyday Life	28
Lasting Legacy	30
Index & Time Line	32

Mesopotamia

This book is about an area of the ancient world called **Mesopotamia**, a name that means "the land between the rivers." The rivers are the Euphrates and the Tigris, and the land between them was home to many different **communities** of people. Today, most of ancient Mesopotamia lies within the borders of Iraq, with small parts in Turkey and Syria. In ancient times, northern Mesopotamia was called Assyria, and the south was called Sumer and, later, Babylonia.

THE LAND AND CLIMATE

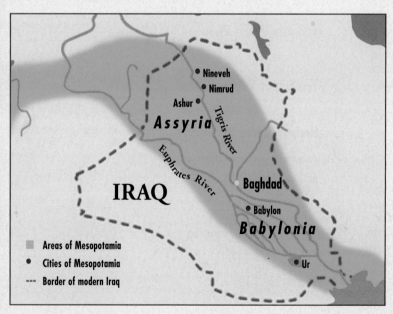

This map shows the main settlements in ancient Mesopotamia.

Map labels:
- Nineveh
- Nimrud
- Ashur
- Assyria
- Tigris River
- Euphrates River
- IRAQ
- Baghdad
- Babylon
- Babylonia
- Ur

Legend:
- Areas of Mesopotamia
- Cities of Mesopotamia
- Border of modern Iraq

The region's climate is hot and **arid** in summer and cold in winter. Dust storms occur frequently, particularly on the flat **floodplains** between the Euphrates and the Tigris.

With such little rainfall, people have always lived close to these two rivers. The specific places they once lived are known today because **archaeologists** have **excavated** the remains of many Mesopotamian villages and cities. Early villages from 8000–6000 B.C. have been excavated, as have the first large cities, which date from about 3500 B.C. From time to time, both rivers changed their courses, cutting new channels across the floodplains. When this happened, settlements were sometimes washed away.

Word Discovery

civilization *a culture and its people*
climate *weather*

culture *customs and beliefs*
settlements *places where people set up communities*

society *highly organized community with common interests and institutions*

WHO WERE THE MESOPOTAMIANS?

There were many different communities of Mesopotamian people. The major groups included the Sumerians (living from 3500 to 1900 B.C.), the Akkadians (2334 to 2150 B.C.), the Babylonians (1792 to 539 B.C.), and the Assyrians (1200 to 612 B.C.). Information about these different communities was gathered from many clay tablets that were discovered in excavations. For example, one clay tablet lists the kings of Sumeria. These first kings were believed to have lived for thousands of years:

*When kingship was lowered from heaven …
A-lulim (became) king and ruled 28,800 years.
Alalgar ruled 36,000 years. Two kings (thus)
ruled it for 64,800 years.**

Assyrian king Ashurnasirpal II and his attendants are pictured on this glazed tile from the Assyrian city of Nimrud, which dates to between 883 and 859 B.C.

*Source: "The Sumerian king list," early-second millennium B.C.

Glossary

archaeologists people who study ancient objects to learn about the past
arid very dry, like a desert
canals waterways cut across land
communities groups of people living together in one area
excavate dig up a site to reveal objects from the past

floodplains flat areas that may be covered with floods
Mesopotamia (meh-sah-pa-tay-mi-ah) ancient name the for area now covered mainly by Iraq
vegetation plants

See also: Nomads to City Dwellers 6–7, The People 8–9, Wars and Weapons 20–21, Farming and Food 22–23

CASE STUDY

King Shalmaneser III is shown discovering the source of the Tigris River in this bronze relief, c. 853 B.C.

Euphrates and Tigris Rivers

People in Mesopotamia depended on the two great rivers. Water flowed from the rivers to farm fields through special **canals** that the people dug across the plains. This method of watering fields is known as irrigation and is still used in the region today. Both the Euphrates River (1,740 miles [2,800 kilometers] long) and the faster-flowing Tigris River (1,180 miles [1,900 km] long) flooded every year between April and June. Writings, such as this wedding blessing, make clear the importance of these rivers in ancient times:

*Into the Tigris and Euphrates may flood water be brought, On their banks may the grass grow high, may the meadows be covered, May the holy queen of **vegetation** pile high the grain heaps and mounds.**

*Source: Anonymous, "Inanna and the King: wedding night blessing," early-2nd millennium B.C.

Nomads to City Dwellers

As the site of some of the world's earliest civilizations, Mesopotamia was where many important cultural developments and inventions were made. One of the earliest and greatest advances in human life was farming. When the Mesopotamians learned how to take plants and animals from the wild and raise them for their own benefit, they no longer needed to live as **nomads**, hunting and gathering food from the wild. Instead, they settled down and became the world's first farmers in the world's first villages.

DOMESTICATING PLANTS

Around 9000 B.C., the Mesopotamians started to **domesticate** two types of wheat called *emmer* and *einkorn* that they found growing in the wild.

With each new harvest, farmers saved seeds from the best plants and sowed, or planted, them the following year. Farmers domesticated other wild plants too. Barley, peas, lentils, carrots, turnips, and leeks were all grown by the early Mesopotamians and their neighbors. Greek writer Herodotus was amazed by Mesopotamian crops:

*Of all the countries that we know there is none which is so fruitful in grain ... As for the **millet** and the sesame, I shall not say to what height they grow, though within my own knowledge; for I am not **ignorant** that what I have already written concerning the fruitfulness of Babylonia must seem incredible to those who have never visited the country.* *

Einkorn, a wild variety of wheat, was one of the first plants the Mesopotamian farmers grew as crops.

*Source: Herodotus, "Histories, Book I," fifth century B.C.

DOMESTICATING ANIMALS

The early Mesopotamians were also the first people to domesticate wild animals. The dog, which is probably the first animal they domesticated, first appeared about 9000 B.C. People chose dogs to live and work with them because dogs were good for hunting. By about 7000 B.C., other wild animals had **evolved** into domesticated breeds, too. Sheep were the first and the most important. Other animals that the Mesopotamians domesticated include the pig and the cow. Because these animals provided food and other resources, people cared a lot about the health and breeding of animals, as shown in this hymn:

My king, the ewe has given birth to the lamb, The ewe has given birth to the lamb, the ewe has given birth to the good sheep, I will pronounce your name again and again. *

This stone vase, decorated with carved sheep, was made about 3400–3200 B.C.

*Source: Hymn to Ninurta as god of fertility and vegetation, second millennium B.C.

Glossary

domesticate adapt a wild plant or animal for life with humans for human benefit
evolved developed or descended from an earlier or simpler form of the same thing
foundation base something stands on
populations numbers of people

ignorant lacking knowledge or awareness
millet type of grain
nomad a person who travels from place to place, usually in seasonal movements
scrutinize look over closely
testify confirm proof of something

CASE STUDY

Ishtar Gate is the main gateway to the inner city of Babylon.

Villages, Towns, and Cities

As the idea and practice of farming spread, villages appeared throughout Mesopotamia. When the villages grew larger, they turned into the world's first towns, including Uruk, which emerged about 3500 B.C. Now located in the desert of southern Iraq, Uruk was discovered by modern people about one hundred years ago. As their **populations** increased, some Mesopotamian towns became the world's first cities. The people of Mesopotamia were proud of their new way of living, as is clear in the words of Gilgamesh, the king of Uruk, as he shows off his city:

*Go on to the wall of Uruk, Ur-shanabi, and walk around, Inspect the **foundation** platform and **scrutinize** the brickwork! **Testify** that its bricks are baked bricks, And that the Seven Counselors must have laid its foundations! ... Three square miles and the open ground comprise Uruk.* *

*Source: "Gilgamesh, Tablet XI," early-1st millennium B.C.

See also: Mesopotamia 4–5, The People 8–9, Farming and Food 22–23, Lasting Legacy 30–31

The People

As towns and cities began to flourish across Mesopotamia, the people who lived in them organized into a highly structured society. Powerful kings ranked at the top of society, and slaves were at the bottom. The great mass of ordinary people fell in between these two groups. Much is known about the way that Mesopotamian society was organized during the time of King Hammurabi, in the eighteenth century B.C., and it is the system in Hammurabi's time that is described here.

KINGS — THE RULERS OF MESOPOTAMIA

There were many different communities of people living in Mesopotamia and, therefore, many different rulers.

This is a bronze bust of King Sargon, ruler of Assyria. It dates from about 1850 B.C. and was found at Nineveh.

Mesopotamian rulers were almost always men. Women were sometimes very powerful but only in association with kings or their own families. When a king died, usually one of his sons became the new king. The eldest son was the likely successor to his father, but sometimes another son or someone else would become king. The king lived in a palace and ranked above everyone in the region except the gods. Many of the kings wrote proud, boastful comments about themselves, such as these words from Shalmaneser III:

*(I am) Shalmaneser, the **legitimate** king, the king of the world, the king without **rival**, the "Great Dragon," the (only) power within the four rims (of the earth), overlord of all the princes, who has smashed all his enemies as if (they be) **earthenware**.*

*Source: Shalmaneser III, "The Fight Against the Aramean Coalition: Reign of Shalmaneser III," ninth century B.C.

Word Discovery

dominant *having control, power, or influence over others*
expanded *made bigger*

humanity *mankind*
matrimony *marriage*
monarch *king or queen*

regulations *laws or rules*
empire *many territories ruled by one person or country*

COMMONERS, SLAVES, AND WOMEN

The Law Code of Hammurabi clearly stated how the Mesopotamian people were ranked. The first class of people were the *awilu,* or landowners. Next came the *mushkenu,* or dependents, who did not own land but farmed the land owned by the awilu. Last of all were the *wardu,* or slaves. Women in Mesopotamia were not considered part of this class system. They could own land, but few did. Although laws generally favored men, it was possible for a wife to divorce her husband:

*If a woman so hated her husband that she has declared, "You may not have me," her record shall be investigated at her city council, and if she was careful and was not at fault, even though her husband has been going out and **disparaging** her greatly, that woman, without incurring any blame at all, may take her **dowry** and go off to her father's house.* *

This terra-cotta statue of a woman is from Babylonia and dates from c. 1900 to 1700 B.C.

*Source: The Law Code of Hammurabi, eighteeth century B.C.

Glossary

devout very religious
disparaging making insulting comments
dowry property or money brought by a bride to her marriage
earthenware pottery

legitimate having rights based on law or heredity
oppress use power to burden
rival someone with qualities of or competing with another

See also: Mesopotamia 4–5, Palaces and Houses 10–11, Writing and Law 18–19, Wars and Weapons 20–21

CASE STUDY

This carved head of King Hammurabi is from Susa, eighteenth century B.C.

Hammurabi, a Famous King

Hammurabi was king of Babylon from 1728 to 1685 B.C. When he became king, Babylon was only one of many small cities in Mesopotamia. Hammurabi did not want to be remembered as a weak leader, so in the last years of his reign he attacked neighboring cities and took their land. Hammurabi became the region's most powerful king, and Babylon became the leading city. Hammurabi did many good things for his people. He is perhaps best remembered for creating a code of laws that were designed to prevent the powerful from taking advantage of the weak. Here is an excerpt from his code of law:

*[The gods] Anum and Enlil named me to promote the welfare of the people, Me, Hammurabi, the **devout**, god-fearing prince, To cause justice to prevail in the land, To destroy the wicked and the evil, That the strong might not **oppress** the weak.* *

*Source: Law Code of Hammurabi, 18th century B.C.

Palaces and Houses

People lived in different types of houses, depending on their status in Mesopotamian society. The king lived in the best home of all — a palace — while his people lived in much smaller houses. Both palaces and houses were made from a building material called **mud-brick**. The ruins of Mesopotamian palaces from several ancient cities still exist, including those at Mari, Babylon, and Nineveh. These ruins, along with ancient writings, give a clear picture of where people lived all those thousands of years ago.

PALACES FOR KINGS

A palace was a sign of power and wealth. Some palaces had two stories, a flat roof, and as many as three hundred rooms.

Some palace rooms were used as **treasuries,** where a king stored his valuables and fortune. Other rooms were workshops, where craftsmen made objects for the monarch. The king met visitors and made announcements in the most important room — the throne room. This room was sometimes decorated with paintings or stone carvings with images of wars or of the king

This photograph shows the ruins of Nebuchadnezzar II's palace (630–562 B.C.) in Babylon, Iraq.

hunting. Kings were proud of their palaces, as is clear in this statement from Tiglath-Pileser III:

(My enemies), whose countries [far away], towards West, [heard] the fame of my rule […and brought]… gold, silver, … camels and all kinds of spices [to me and kis]sed my feet … I estab[lished] a palace as be[fitting for my position as their king].*

*Source: "Campaigns Against Syria & Palestine," 8th century B.C.

HOUSES FOR COMMONERS

This Assyrian relief shows builders at work in a village. It comes from the Palace of Sargon at Khorsabad, c. 721–705 B.C.

relaxed in the **courtyard**. Only rich people could afford bathrooms and toilets, which drained into the river. Most houses, and even the palaces of kings, were built from sun-dried mud-bricks that were good for keeping out the heat. Houses had one door to the street, sometimes with the frame painted red to keep out evil spirits. The following ancient **agreement** describes some details of renting a house:

Most people lived in small, cube-shaped houses. Rooms downstairs were for working and receiving visitors. Bedrooms and dining rooms were upstairs. Families cooked their meals and

*A … house belonging to Nana-iddina … [is] at the **disposal** of Anu-uballit … for 4 **shekels** of silver as the rent of the house per year … The bareness [of the walls] he shall **rectify**; the cracks of the walls he shall close up.* *

*Source: Rent-of-House Document, late-Babylonian period

Glossary

agreement legally binding document; act of agreeing
courtyard an open-air space next to a building
disposal have authority to use
mud-brick a rectangular brick made from mud that has dried hard

rectify fix a problem
shekel silver coin used as money in Mesopotamia
treasuries places where stores of money or valuable property is kept

See also: Mesopotamia 4–5, The People 8–9, Farming and Food 22–23, Everyday Life 28–29

CASE STUDY

Some people believe these ruins in Iraq are the foundations of the Hanging Gardens of Babylon. Other people believe the gardens never existed.

Hanging Gardens of Babylon

The most famous royal palace was built in the city of Babylon by King Nebuchadnezzar II, who reigned from 630 to 562 B.C. The palace is best known today for its so-called Hanging Gardens. Greek writer Philo named the gardens as one of the Seven Wonders of the World. He wrote :

The Hanging Garden with its plants above the ground grows in the air. The roots of trees above form a roof over the ground. Stone pillars stand under the garden to support it. *

Some people think the story of the Hanging Gardens is a myth. It remains an unsolved mystery.

*Source: Philo, third century B.C.

Religion

The Mesopotamians were a highly religious people and worshiped many different gods and goddesses. They believed people had been created to serve the gods and to work for them as their servants on Earth. Mesopotamians thought that if they served the gods well, they would be protected from harm. They also believed, however, that if they did not look after the gods, bad things might happen, such as floods, **drought**, disease, or attacks from their enemies.

GODS AND GODDESSES

Ancient people believed gods and goddesses were immortal beings with **superhuman** powers.

As many as three thousand different **deities** were worshiped in Mesopotamia, although not all of them by the same communities. Many written tributes to the gods survive, such as the **Hymn** to Ishtar:

Praise Ishtar, the most awesome of the goddesses … The fate of everything she holds in her hand. At her glance there is created joy, Power, magnificence, the protecting deity and guardian spirit. *

This double statue is of God Adad and Goddess Ishtar and is from the ninth century B.C. It was discovered at Tell Halaf, an archaeological site in Syria.

*Source: "Hymn to Ishtar," 1600 B.C.

Word Discovery

afterlife *another life and world beyond this one*
ceremony *formal event*

performed according to ritual
divine *relating to or coming from a god*

pious *very religious*
ritual *the words or acts performed in a ceremony*

HYMNS AND PRAYERS

Priests composed hymns, which were sacred songs that praised the gods and thanked them for their kindness. Many of these hymns still survive on written clay tablets. Hymns were spoken or sung to music played on instruments, such as the harp. Prayers were offered to the gods for many different reasons. People with poor health asked to be made better, those with enemies asked to be kept safe from harm, those with no food asked to be fed, and so on. Here is a portion of one Mesopotamian hymn:

> *O my god, (my)* **transgressions**
> *are seven times seven; remove my transgressions; O my goddess, (my) transgressions are seven times seven; remove my transgressions; … Remove my transgressions and I will sing thy praise.* *

Sumerian statuette of a person in prayer

*Source: "Prayer to Every God," seventh century B.C.

Glossary

deities gods or goddesses
drought a long period of time without rainfall
hymn religious song praising a god or giving thanks
superhuman having abilities greater than a normal human
transgressions the breaking of rules or laws; not meeting one's duties

CASE STUDY

This limestone plaque showing people bearing offerings to the gods comes from Ur in southern Iraq and dates to between 2500 and 2300 B.C.

Holy Days and Festivals

Certain days were holy days or times when religious festivals were held. These festivals were important events at which the gods were praised and celebrated. In return for their public displays of love, respect, and loyalty, people hoped the gods would protect their towns and provide them with food. Many holy days and festivals were connected with farming, such as the festival of *akitu*, a thanksgiving festival for the barley harvest and a celebration for the start of a new year. Here is a portion of a temple purification ceremony performed at Babylon during this New Year festival:

> *When it is two hours after sunrise, … purify the temple and sprinkle water, (taken from) … the Tigris and … the Euphrates, on the temple. He [the priest] shall beat the kettle-drum inside the temple. He shall have a censer and a torch brought into the temple …* *

*Source: Temple program for the New Year's festival at Babylon, third century B.C.

See also: Palaces and Houses 10–11, Temples and Ziggurats 14–15, Mythology 16–17, Science and Medicine 26–27

Temples and Ziggurats

Every Mesopotamian town and city had at least one **temple** building and sometimes many of them. A temple was built in honor of the community's main god and was a very important place. As the years passed, a temple was developed into multiple religious buildings spread out over a large area. Some of these temple **complexes** contained another important building — a pyramid-shaped tower called a *ziggurat*.

TEMPLES

A Mesopotamian temple was not a meeting place for worshipers. Instead, the people believed that it was a house on Earth where the spirit of a god lived:

*Bright light, god Marduk, who dwells in the temple Eudul, … To your city, Babylon, grant release! … At your **exalted** command, O lord of the great gods, Let light be set before the people of Babylon.**

In addition to the temple building, a temple complex included living areas for priests and temple workers. Worshipers gathered in the complex's open-air courtyards on holy days and during festivals, and valuables and grain were kept safe in storerooms. A temple was a busy place, with people coming and going all day. The entire temple complex was surrounded by a high wall.

The ziggurat at Ur is the most famous example of a Mesopotamian ziggurat.

*Source: Temple program for the New Year's festival at Babylon, third century B.C.

Word Discovery

dedicated *devoted to*
magnificent *grand*
monument *a building erected*

to the memory of a person or event
protocol *rules of behavior*

sanctuary *holiest place in a temple*
significant *very important*

ZIGGURATS

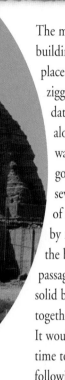

This is the ziggurat at Aqarquf, near Baghdad.

The most famous type of Mesopotamian building is the ziggurat, which means "high place." One of the best examples of a ziggurat, the one at Ur in southern Iraq, dates from 2000 B.C. A ziggurat stood alone or within a temple complex and was thought of as a ladder leading to the gods. It was a pyramid-shaped tower of several flat platforms, built one on top of the other. The platforms were reached by ramps and staircases on the outside of the building. There were no rooms or passages inside a ziggurat. Instead, it was a solid block of millions of mud-bricks held together with wooden beams and reed matting. It would have taken the Mesopotamians a long time to build a ziggurat, as is clear from the following passage:

*The Annunaki [people] began shoveling, For a whole year they made bricks for it, When the second year arrived, … They had built a high ziggurat.**

*Source: "The Epic of Creation, Tablet VI," early-second millennium B.C.

Glossary

complex something made up of related parts, such as a group of buildings
deity a god or goddess
exalted of a very high rank
sacrifice offer something of value to a god, including killing an animal

temple building for worshiping or honoring a god or gods
ziggurat pyramid-shaped structure with steps up its sides that lead to flat platforms and a temple

CASE STUDY

This figure of a temple priest is from the Palace of Sargon at Khorsabad.

Priests and Priestesses

Priests were men, and they tended to work at temples dedicated to gods. Priestesses were women, and they usually worked at temples dedicated to goddesses. Both groups had shaved heads, which was a sign of cleanliness. Their duty was to serve the **deity** of the temple where they worked. Twice a day they took gifts of food to the sacred statue, where the god or goddess was believed to live, and dressed it in clean clothes. At festivals, they paraded the statue in the courtyard for worshipers to see. Sometimes they carried the statue to temples in other towns, so their god could visit other gods. Priests and priestesses also **sacrificed** animals to the gods:

*Every day throughout the year, ten fat, clean rams, whose horns and hooves are whole, shall be sacrificed … to the deities Anu and Antu of heaven, to the planets Jupiter, Venus, Mercury, Saturn, and Mars, to the sunrise, and to the appearance of the moon.**

*Source: "Daily sacrifices to the gods of the city of Uruk," third century B.C.

See also: Palaces and Houses 10–11, Religion 12–13, Mythology 16–17, Science and Medicine 26–27

Mythology

The Mesopotamians told many different stories about their gods and heroes. These stories are called **myths**, but the people in Mesopotamia believed that their stories about gods, magic, and strange creatures were true. At first, these stories were passed on by word-of-mouth. In time, however, they were written down, and many have survived and can be read today.

The head of a horned dragon was the symbol of Marduk. This bronze sculpture is from sixth century B.C. Babylonia.

THE EPIC OF CREATION

young god Marduk. He agrees to join the fight on the condition that if he wins he will be made the **supreme** god. Marduk forces Tiamat to swallow the wind, and her body inflates like a balloon. He shoots an arrow into her, and she bursts open and dies. Marduk opens Tiamat's eyes, and the Euphrates and Tigris Rivers flow from them. He makes rain, wind, and clouds from her spit, fog from her poison, and mountains from her breasts. He creates the stars and the moon. Lastly, he creates people from the blood of the monster Kingu. Here is an excerpt from the story:

*Face to face they came, Tiamat and Marduk …To her face he dispatched the imhullu-wind, … Tiamat opened her mouth to swallow it, And he forced in the imhullu wind so that she could not close her lips … He shot an arrow which pierced her belly, Split her down the middle and slit her heart, **Vanquished** her and extinguished her life.**

In the story "The Epic of Creation," Mesopotamians celebrated Marduk, the city god of Babylon, whom they believed created the first people.

The story begins with a group of old gods, led by the goddess Tiamat, fighting a great battle among themselves. Into this chaos steps the

*Source: "The Epic of Creation," second millennium B.C.

Word Discovery

carnage *great bloodshed*
celestial *relating to heaven or outer space*

epic *long poem about hero; art or events of great length*
grotesque *ugly*

immortality *living forever*
moral *related to principles of right and wrong behavior*

THE EPIC OF GILGAMESH

This stone relief of hero Gilgamesh, with a lion under one arm and a sword in the other hand, is from Khorsabad, eighth century B.C.

"The Epic of Gilgamesh" is the tale of Gilgamesh, a historical king of Uruk in 2700 B.C., and his search for eternal life. His search leads him to Ut-napishtim, who tells him about a great flood that almost destroyed humankind. Ut-napishtim was saved because he built a great boat for himself, his family, and all the animals of the world. When he released a raven and it did not fly back, he knew the bird must have found dry land. In thanks, Ut-napishtim offered sacrifices to the gods, and, in return, the god Enlil gave him **eternal** life. Echoes of his tale survive in the Bible story of Noah and the flood. As for Gilgamesh, he failed to gain eternal life, and in this excerpt from the story, a woman named Siduri warns him against his quest:

Gilgamesh, where do you roam? You will not find the eternal life you seek. When the gods created mankind, They appointed death for mankind, Kept eternal life in their own hands.*

*Source: "Gilgamesh" (Old Babylonian version), early-second millennium B.C.

Glossary

demon evil spirit or devil
eternal never ending
impetuous acting without thinking
intestines digestive part of a body
myths traditional stories about supposed

historical events that try to explain beliefs, practices, or the natural world
supreme highest rank or quality
vanquished defeated in a battle or contest

CASE STUDY

This clay mask of the demon Humbaba is from Sippar in southern Iraq, c. 1800–1600 B.C.

Demons and Monsters

Mesopotamians believed in the existence of **demons** and monsters, many of whom appear in their stories. Demons acted as agents of the gods, sent to Earth to punish people, and monsters were hideous creatures. The giant monster Humbaba, for example, had a face that looked like a coiled mass of sheep's **intestines**. According to the ancient story "Epic of Gilgamesh," Humbaba was killed when Gilgamesh chopped off his head. In the following quote, the elders of Uruk warn Gilgamesh about the dangers of Humbaba:

*You are (still young), Gilgamesh, you are **impetuous** ... But you do not know what you will find ... Humbaba, whose shout is the flood weapon, Whose utterance is fire and whose breath is death, Can hear for up to sixty leagues the sound of his forest.**

*Source: "Gilgamesh" (Standard version), early-first millennium B.C.

See also: Religion 12–13, Temples and Ziggurats 14–15, Writing and Law 18–19, Everyday Life 28–29

Writing and Law

Writing was invented by the Sumerians, who lived in southern Mesopotamia in about 3000 B.C. Their brilliant invention was a milestone in the history of humankind and allowed the Mesopotamian culture to make great progress. Using their surviving writings, we can learn much about the Mesopotamians directly through the power of their own words. Their texts range from simple lists of goods to complex stories and the laws that governed the way their society was run.

PICTURES AND SOUNDS

This necklace bead bears a cuneiform inscription that says it belonged to Mesanepada, King of Hur Mari, c. 2500 B.C.

The Mesopotamians first wrote using a type of picture- writing. This method used pictures to represent things.

These kinds of pictures are called *pictograms*. A picture of a sheep meant "one sheep," while a sheep with two circles beside it meant "two sheep." This type of writing was invented to record the business activities of farmers and merchants. Writing with pictograms was limited, however, because they could be used only for object words and not for all the words in the Mesopotamian language. Other words were written as symbols. Such symbols are called *phonograms*. Writing continued to develop to help keep financial and administrative records, such as this one from a temple document:

*Marduk-remani the scribe … has received 23 kur 5 sut of dates as a partial payment from the hands of Arad-Bel … (he) has entered this partial payment … on the writing board … and will show it to Iddin-Bel and Nabu-eber-napshati.**

*Source: Temple administrative document (payment for scribe Marduk-remani), fifth–fourth century B.C.

Word Discovery

chronicle *written account of historical events*
composition *a piece of writing*

inventory *a detailed list*
literacy *being able to read and write*

legal *lawful or relating to the law*
nouns *words that name things*

WRITING ON CLAY

Mesopotamians did not write on paper. Instead, they wrote on pieces of soft clay that are called clay **tablets** today. To write on clay, a **scribe** held a tablet in the palm of one hand. The back of the tablet was rounded to fit the hollow of his palm. The face of the tablet was flat and was what the scribe wrote on with a **stylus** made from the cut stem of a water reed. A scribe wrote in lines running from left to right or from top to bottom. When he had finished, the tablet was dried in the sun or baked hard in an oven. This writing looks like clusters of wedge-shaped marks. The name given to this kind of

Mesopotamian wedge-writing is **cuneiform**, which is Latin for "wedge-shaped."

This thirteenth century B.C. clay tablet from El Quitar, Syria (top) shows the cuneiform script. The clay outer envelope (bottom) protected the contents from being altered.

Glossary

cuneiform Mesopotamian writing using wedge-shaped characters
phonogram symbol representing a word, syllable, or sound
pictogram picture that acts as a symbol for an object
scribe professional writer
stylus writing instrument used by ancient people for writing on clay or wax tablets
tablets flat slabs or sets of sheets used for writing

CASE STUDY

Law

Mesopotamian laws were often written on clay tablets. They were also carved on blocks of stone that were put up in public places for everyone to see. Most people could not read or write, however, and so important documents would be read aloud to crowds of people. The most famous Mesopotamian set of laws is the Law Code of Hammurabi. This code is a list of 282 laws that were carved in thirty-five hundred lines of cuneiform writing onto a block of hard black stone. The stone is about 8 feet (2.5 meters) tall and weighs 4.4 tons (4 tonnes). Hammurabi's laws were organized into sections dealing with family, work, property, land, prices and wages, slavery, and trade. The laws were designed to be fair to all but included many harsh punishments. Here are three examples of these laws:

*If a son hits his father, his hand shall be cut off; ... If a man puts out a man's eye, his own eye shall be put out; ... If a man breaks a man's bone, he shall pay him a sum of silver.**

The Law Code of Hammurabi was inscribed on this plaque from Chaldea in the eighth century B.C.

See also: The People 18–19, Arts and Crafts 24–25, Science and Medicine 26–27, Lasting Legacy 30–31

*Source: Law Code of Hammurabi, 18th century B.C.

Wars and Weapons

Wars were fought throughout the history of Mesopotamia. Conflicts usually began when one community did something to offend another. For example, if a city tried to take control of another city's water supply, the two might go to war. Other reasons for fighting might be a king's invading his neighbor's land, stealing or damaging his property, or insulting his gods. In a land where access to water was essential for growing crops, many conflicts occurred over water rights.

THE ARMY

King Sargon of Akkad (who reigned from 2234 to 2279 B.C.) formed the first army of full-time soldiers. The army included men who fought at close range with spears and swords, archers who fired arrows from a distance, messengers, and spies. The army employed **engineers** who built equipment, such as battering-rams to break down the walls of enemy cities. Fortune-tellers were also part of the army. Their job was to sacrifice animals and inspect their **entrails**, looking for **omens** about the success or failure of the king's military plan.

Much of the information about ancient Mesopotamian warfare comes from spectacular carved stone slabs from palaces in cities, such as Nineveh and Nimrud. Kings also wrote many descriptions of the wars they fought:

As to Hanno of Gaza … who had fled before my army and run away to Egypt, [I conquered] the town of Gaza … [and I placed the images of] my [gods] and my royal image in his own palace … and declared [them] to be … the gods of their country.*

The Royal Standard of Ur is one of the earliest images of the Sumerian army, including their chariots.

*Source: Tiglath-pileser III, 744–727 B.C.

Word Discovery

campaigns *the preparation for battles and the battles themselves*

expedition *trip taken for a specific purpose*
formidable *inspiring fear*

or caution
siege *an army surrounding its enemy until they surrender*

WEAPONS AND ARMOR

The main weapons used by the Mesopotamian armies were the spear and the bow and arrow. Other weapons included spears, javelins, axes, maces, daggers, slings, and swords with long, curved blades. Soldiers wore leather or metal helmets to protect their heads. Metal armor was made from hundreds of tiny pieces of bronze that overlapped each other, like fish scales, and were sewn to a leather or cloth tunic. Mesopotamian weapons are clearly described by Greek writer Herodotus:

The Assyrians went to war with helmets upon their heads made of brass, and plaited in a strange fashion which is not easy to describe. They carried shields, **lances***, and daggers very like the Egyptian; but in addition they had wooden clubs knotted with iron, and linen* **corselets***.* *

This copper axe (left) was found in one of the royal graves of Ur and is from about 2600 to 2400 B.C. The bronze sword (above) is from the Kassite dynasty, 1400-1100 B.C.

*Source: Herodotus, "Histories," fifth century B.C.

Glossary

bespattered covered by splashing
corselets type of armor
engineers people who design and build things
entrails inside parts of an animal

lances long, spearlike weapons
omen a sign believed to predict a future event
stele stone with an inscription or design used as a marker

CASE STUDY

This eighth-century B.C. basalt Assyrian stele from Tell Ahamr shows warriors riding in a chariot.

The Chariot

Two-wheeled chariots were an important feature of Mesopotamian armies. Fast and lightweight, they were the chief fighting vehicle of their time. A chariot was a platform on wheels pulled by horses and steered by a driver. An archer fired arrows from the platform. Some chariots held up to four archers. Chariots could also carry a bodyguard whose job was to hold a shield in front of the archer to protect him. Chariots were also used on hunting trips. Sennacherib described his bloody ride on a chariot in a war against Elam:

My prancing steeds, harnessed for my riding, plunged into the streams of their blood ... The wheels of my war chariot ... were **bespattered** *with blood and filth.**

*Source: "Annals of Sennacherib," late-eighth century B.C.

Farming and Food

Farmers were very important to Mesopotamian society. More people worked the land — growing crops, tending to animals, and looking after the water supply — than in any other occupation. In the northern region, farmers relied on rainfall to water their fields. In the drier south, water was **channeled** to fields through **irrigation** canals. Digging and clearing canals were extremely important public duties for all citizens, in order to make their lands more **fertile**.

CROPS, BREAD, AND BEER

The farmers' most important crop was barley. They ground the barley grains into flour to make bread.

Milk, butter, cheese, fruit, and sesame seeds were added to flour to make different kinds of bread. People also used barley to make a low-alcohol beer that they drank through straws to avoid swallowing solid pieces of grain. Their main vegetables were onions and garlic, along with lettuces, cabbages, carrots, and cucumbers. Fruit crops included apples, cherries, figs, pears, plums, and dates. Water was crucial to farmers for growing everything, as shown in this excerpt from a list of farmers' instructions:

*In days of yore a farmer gave (these) instructions to his son: When you are about to **cultivate** your field, take care to open the irrigation works (so that) their water does not rise too high in the field. When you have emptied it of water, watch the field's wet ground that it stays even: let no wandering ox trample it.**

In this detail of the Warka Vase from Uruk, dated 3500 to 3000 B.C., men are shown carrying food.

*Source: Farmer's Instructions, 1700 B.C.

Word Discovery

livelihood *way of providing what's needed to live*
orchard *group of fruit trees*

staple *main food in a society*
seasoning *something that adds flavor, such as spices or herbs*

added to food
trapping *catching animals in traps or cages*

ANIMALS

This terra-cotta seal from the second millennium B.C. is from the Syrian city of Mari and shows a man with deer. These animals would have been hunted for their meat.

The main farm animals were sheep and goats (which provided milk) and cattle. Farmers sheared sheep for the wool and made cattle hides into leather, using both materials to make clothes. Mesopotamians ate the meat of pigs, sheep, deer, and cattle, and raised ducks, geese, and hens for eggs and meat. The main **draft** animals, oxen and donkeys, were used to pull carts and plows and for other projects around the farm:

Once the sky constellations are right, do not be reluctant to take the oxen force to the field many times.*

*Source: "Farmer's Almanac," 1700 B.C.

Glossary

channeled directed along a specific path, such as in a canal
cultivate prepare and use for growing crops or plants
draft team of animals used for

pulling something
fertile good for farming (land)
irrigation channeling water to crops
preserved treated so that it does not spoil (food)

See also: Mesopotamia 4–5, Nomads to City Dwellers 6–7, Everyday Life 28–29

CASE STUDY

Fishing and Hunting

In addition to what they grew on farms, Mesopotamians also ate wild food, especially fish. People fished on the Tigris and Euphrates Rivers, in lakes, and in the Mediterranean and Gulf Seas. Teams of fishermen trapped fish in large nets and pulled them ashore. Other people worked alone, hooking fish with rods and lines or with small nets. Fish was eaten fresh or was **preserved** by salting or smoking. Hunters added hares, birds, and gazelles to meals. People in Babylon even caught locusts, which they enjoyed as a crunchy insect delicacy.

The sea was filled with carp and ... fish, ... The forests were filled with deer and wild goats, ... The watered gardens were filled with (honey) and wine.*

Men hunting with dogs and cages are depicted in this Assyrian relief from Nineveh, dated about 650 B.C.

*Source: "Hymn to Ninurta as god of fertility and vegetation," second millennium B.C.

Arts and Crafts

The people of Mesopotamia who made crafts used a wide range of raw materials. They made ordinary everyday items, luxury goods, and art objects. It is believed that craft workers were always men, and that fathers passed on their skills to their sons, from one generation to the next. Studying the objects these ancient people made can reveal to modern man how the items were made, the tools used to make them, and something about the society from which they came.

METAL OBJECTS

Copper, bronze, and iron were the main metals used to make everyday objects, such as kitchen equipment, weapons, statues, and parts for chariots and furniture.

Craftsmen used gold and silver for decorative and high-quality items, such as jewelery. Mesopotamia lacked the **ores** needed to produce metals, so these materials had to be brought in from other regions. Workers poured hot, melted copper and bronze into **molds** of clay or stone to **cast** axes, daggers, and spearheads. They also used casting for gold and silver items. Iron needed higher temperatures and could not be shaped by casting. Instead, workers heated iron in a **forge**, then beat it into shape. Craftsmen also made special vessels from precious metals that were used for offering food to the gods:

*Every day in the year, for the main meal of the morning, you shall prepare … eighteen gold **vessels** … (filled with various kinds of beer) on the tray of the god Anu**

This gold headdress is from the Royal Cemetery at Ur, from about 2600 B.C.

*Source: "Daily Sacrifices to the Gods of the City of Uruk," second millennium B.C.

Word Discovery

artisan *skilled worker who makes things by hand*
elaborate *detailed*

molten *melted; something made by melting and casting*
pendant *piece of jewelery*

that hangs from a necklace
technique *method*

CLAY, GLASS, AND IVORY

Pottery making was the most common Mesopotamian craft. Clay — pottery's raw material – was found across the region, and potters shaped it into bowls, plates, saucers, and jars. The first pots were handmade. Later, after about 4500 B.C., pots were made on a slowly spinning wheel that allowed potters to make pots in different shapes. Glass-making was very skilled work. About 1600 B.C., the Mesopotamians learned how to make hollow glass objects, such as vases and bottles. Many fine objects and raw materials came into Mesopotamian cities as war **booty**:

*I carried away as booty his ... possessions in large amounts ... gold, silver, precious stones, elephant-hides, **ivory**, ebony and boxwood, garments (made) with multicolored trimmings and linen, all his personal valuables**

Dating back to the Kassite dynasty (about 1300–1200 B.C.), this glass bottle was found in a grave at Ur.

*Source: Esarhaddon, "Syro–Palestinian Campaign," 680–669 B.C.

Glossary

booty property stolen in wars
cylinder object with straight sides and a circular bottom
cast shape an object by pouring a liquid into a mold and letting it harden
forge a furnace in which metal is heated until it is soft enough to shape

ivory a hard, creamy-white material that comes from elephant tusks
mold a hollow frame in which an object is cast
ore a mineral containing a valuable metal
vessel hollow container for holding a liquid or solid

CASE STUDY

Objects Made of Stone

Stonemasons carved life-size statues of kings and scenes of hunts and battles that decorated the walls of royal palaces. Stone was also used for **cylinder** seals, which were tiny cylinder-shaped objects with finely carved surfaces. When rolled over a clay pad that was fixed to an item of property, a cylinder seal left an impression, or print, of its pattern. The pattern was a *signature* stamp that identified the owner of the property. Here are Assyrian king Sennacherib's instructions for the making of his seal:

You will write ... upon the (stone) tablet-seal ... as follows: Palace of Sennacherib, king... Who(ever) effaces my inscribed name, ... may the gods Ashur, Sin, Shamash, Adad (and) Ishtar ... remove his descendants from the land of stone.*

This white and cream cylinder seal from Uruk in southern Iraq is from c. 3200 to 3100 B.C.

*Source: Sennacherib, "Instructions for inscribing his seal," 714–681 B.C.

See also: Writing and Law 18–19, Wars and Weapons 20–21, Farming and Food 22–23, Everyday Life 28–29

Science and Medicine

The Mesopotamians were interested in the world around them, and they searched for ways to understand and explain it. Evidence that they studied mathematics, **astronomy**, and medicine has been found in the ancient clay tablets on which the Mesopotamians wrote about and explored different ideas about many subjects. Priests usually carried out scientific studies, and they interpreted what they saw in relation to the gods.

MATHEMATICS AND NUMERACY

This is a clay tablet that shows an account of goats and sheep. It comes from Tellohc, Sumeria, c. 2350 B.C.

Mathematics developed in Mesopotamia beginning in about 3000 B.C., soon after the invention of writing.

This new advancement sprang from their need to keep accurate numbers for such things as the amount of grain produced and how many sheep a farmer owned. Their most widely used number system was based on counting in units of sixty. This is called a *sexagesimal* system. They also invented another counting system that was based on counting in tens, hundreds, and thousands. This is called a *decimal* system and is still used today. One everyday use of mathematics was their calculation of rations of food:

A certain Buzi [name] at 120 qu, 4 workmen at 60 qu, 2 female slaves at 30 qu, 2 sons at 30 qu, 2 sons at 20 qu, 2 daughters at 20 qu, [making] 1 kur 260 qu of barley for rations per month. *

*Source: Receipt of barley for rations, early second millennium B.C.

Word Discovery

exorcise *drive out an evil spirit*
numerical *related to numbers*
occult *become concealed, as in*
an eclipse; related to magic
ointment *lotion or cream for*
rubbing on the body
planetary *related to*
the planets
prophecy *a prediction*

ASTRONOMY AND ASTROLOGY

The Sumerians were the first people to describe the Milky Way.

To the Mesopotamians, astronomy and **astrology** were closely related. Priests observed the night sky with the naked eye because they had no telescopes. They kept detailed records of the positions of stars, planets, and the phases of the moon. They believed that the positions of the stars and planets served as **omens** for people on Earth. People made many astronomical observations :

From the 15th day of the (3rd) month Simanu daylight converts to night-time, the days become shorter, the nights become longer,*

But they often explained what they saw in terms of the gods:

*Holy Inanna was **endowed** by Enlil and Ninlil with the power to turn light to darkness and darkness to light.**

*Source: Old Babylonian Document about Inanna, early-second millennium B.C.

Glossary

astrology the study of how stars and
planets influence people's lives
astronomy the science of stars, planets,
and space
decimal a system of counting based on
units of ten
endowed given natural ability

incantation a set of words spoken or
sung as a magic spell
minerals natural substances from the
ground, such as stone, coal, or salt
omens signs which tell the future
sexagesimal a system of counting based
on units of sixty

CASE STUDY

Medicine and Magic

When people got sick, they chose to be seen either by an *asu,* a medical doctor, or an *ashipu,* a doctor who used magic. The ashipu doctor sometimes used spells and **incantations** to heal. The asu doctor made medicines from plants and **minerals**. Here is an asu's, or medical doctor's, cure for pain in the ears:

If the inside of the ears of a man hurt ... you prepare a perfume (using) separately oil from kanaktu, oil from 'sweet-reed', cypress oil, and mix them together, you apply it into his ear, (and then) you wrap a lump of salt in a wad of wool and put it into his ear.*

The "stone tablet of Gula" depicts Gula, the goddess of medicine. It comes from Susa, Iran, and dates to about 1300 B.C.

See also: Religion 12–13, Temples and Ziggurats 14–15, Writing and Law 18–19, Lasting Legacy 30–31

*Source: Medical text, sixth century B.C.

Everyday Life

A variety of evidence survives today that helps paint a picture of everyday life in Mesopotamia. Excavations have uncovered childhood toys and games, while statues, wall carvings, and decorative objects give an idea of the type of clothes people wore. Archaeologists have discovered many musical instruments and even the world's oldest examples of "sheet music," so that the type of music the Mesopotamians liked is known.

TOYS AND GAMES

Babies shook rattles made of baked clay filled with pebbles. Older children played with wooden balls, skipping ropes and spinning tops, and models of animals, furniture, and chariots.

Older children also played with a *buzzer* toy, which was a clay disc with two holes through it, similar to a big button. Children passed a string through the holes and held it at each end, twisting the string until it was **taut**. When the tension was released, the string unwound and the disc whirled around at a speed that made a buzzing noise. Adults liked to play board games. A game for two players was found in a royal tomb in the city of Ur. Made in about 2500 B.C., it is a board of 20 squares. It was a *passing* game. Each player had to move seven counters past his or her opponent's to reach the opposite end of the board.

The Royal Game of Ur dates to about 2600–2400 B.C. and is the most ancient board game known.

Word Discovery

chorus *large group of singers* **cosmetics** *makeup* **fashionable** *stylish*
compose *write music* **entertainment** *fun* **recreation** *hobby*

CLOTHING, HAIR, AND MAKEUP

In about 2500 B.C., men wore short, plain kilts held in place at the hip by a belt or a knot and left their chests bare. Women wore long tunics, wrapped around the body and pinned at the chest. One thousand years later, men wore tunics that reached their knees or ankles, as did women, who also wore shawls to cover their shoulders. In early times, clothes were made from wool. Later, linen became their main fabric. A woman named Lamassi, who sold clothing material, protests against a customer complaint in the letter excerpt below:

Why do you keep on writing to me: "the textiles that you send me are always of bad quality!" Who is the man who lives in your house and criticizes the textiles that are brought to him?*

By 1000 B.C., it was fashionable for men and women to wear their hair in long, tight curls. Men had pointed beards. Women wore makeup, such as **antimony** for mascara and eyeliner and red **henna** for lipstick and blush.

This limestone statuette of a bearded man wearing a tunic is from Tell Asmar, Iraq, and the third millennium B.C.

*Source: Letter written by Lamassi, early-second millennium B.C.

Glossary

antimony brittle blue-black metal used for making women's makeup

castanets small pieces of wood or ivory clicked together with the fingers to make music

cymbals brass plates struck with a stick to make music

henna a reddish-brown dye obtained from the henna plant

lyre a string instrument with two upright posts (a harp has one post only)

taut pulled tight

CASE STUDY

This lyre was found in Queen Pu-abi's grave at the royal cemetery at Ur. It dates from about 2600–2400 B.C.

Music and Song

Clay tablets have been found with musical notes written on them — the world's oldest examples of sheet music. People played music on harps and **lyres** (stringed instruments); pipes, flutes, and horns (wind instruments); and drums, **cymbals**, **castanets**, bells, and rattles (percussion instruments). People sang songs about love and work and hymns that praised the gods. Even Mesopotamian myths were put to music and sung. An ancient table gives advice for tuning a sammu-harp:

If the sammu is tuned to X and the (interval) Y is not clear, you tighten the string N and Y will be clear.*

*Source: Document from Ur, second millennium B.C.

See also: The People 8–9, Palaces and Houses 10–11, Farming and Food 22–23, Arts and Crafts 24–25

Lasting Legacy

The origin of many things in today's world can be traced back to Mesopotamia, including farming methods, writing, and cities. The Mesopotamians also left behind many stories, such as their tale of Ut-napishtim, who also appears in the Bible's Book of Genesis, where he is called Noah. Even the Bible story of the first Christmas can be linked to this ancient civilization, because the three wise men, or *magi*, who traveled from the east were probably Mesopotamian astronomer-priests.

THE INVENTION OF THE WHEEL

The Mesopotamians invented the wheel – one of the greatest inventions in human history. The earliest wheels were probably pottery-spun wheels that date back to about 4700 B.C.

The first wheeled vehicles used wheels that were solid and made from two or three wooden planks shaped into disks. These planks were joined together with wooden or copper **brackets**. People used solid wheels for more than one thousand years in Mesopotamia, until about 2000 B.C. They then began to make lighter wheels that had spokes. As wheeled vehicles became the main means of transportation, roads developed between towns and cities, on which oxen pulled carts. Roads also allowed kings and their armies to move around more quickly, making war and demanding **tribute**:

I departed from Carchemish, taking the road between the mountains ... I advanced towards the town Hazazu ... There I received gold and linen garments (as tribute). *

This chariot model comes from the city of Ur and the Babylonian period (about 2000–1600 B.C.).

*Source: Ashurnasirpal II, 883–859 B.C.

COUNTING IN 60'S

The Mesopotamian counting unit of sixty is still used today. For example, when we measure time we count 60 seconds in a minute and 60 minutes in an hour. Dividing the day into twelve daytime hours and twelve night-time hours is also thought to have been a Mesopotamian invention. In geometry (the branch of mathematics that deals with lines, angles, and solids), we divide a circle into 360 equal parts or degrees, which is a multiple of 60 (6 x 60 = 360).

*The division of the day into twelve parts (was) adopted by the Greeks from the Babylonians.**

The Mesopotamians introduced the legacy of timekeeping as we know it. This seventeenth-century German calender watch shows the days of the week, months, zodiac, and phases of the moon in Arabic symbols.

*Source: Herodotus, "Histories, Book II," fifth century B.C.

CASE STUDY

Mesopotamians invented the twelve signs of the Zodiac still used today.

The Zodiac

The Mesopotamians were avid stargazers and kept detailed records on clay tablets of the movements of stars and planets across the night sky. In about 500 B.C., Mesopotamian astronomer-priests divided the night sky into twelve equal parts and identified each part by a different star **constellation**, giving birth to the **zodiac**. The constellations that they recognized form the basis of modern-day star-signs and **horoscopes**. Just as some people today believe that horoscopes can predict the future, so did the Mesopotamians:

*O great ones, gods of the night, …
O Pleiades, Orion, and the dragon,
O Ursa major, goat (star), and the bison, Stand by, and then, In the divination which I am making,
In the lamb which I am offering,
Put truth for me.**

*Source: Prayer to the gods of the night, early-second millennium B.C.

Glossary

bracket board that runs between and is fixed to two things
constellation a group of stars that form a pattern
divination seeking knowledge through omens
horoscopes predictions of people's future using the stars

magi three wise men from the east who bought gifts to the infant Jesus
tribute payment made by one state or ruler to another when losing a fight or to be protected
zodiac twelve groups of stars, each of which is linked to a human or animal figure and basis for astrology

Index

animals (and animal
 sacrifices) 6, 7, 15, 17,
 20, 22
Assyria(ns) 4, 5, 8, 11, 21, 23
astronomy/astrology 26, 27,
 30, 31

Babylon/Babylonia(ns) 4, 5,
 6, 7, 9, 10, 11, 13, 14,
 16, 23, 30, 31, 32
beer 22, 24
bread 22-23
bricks 7, 10, 11, 15
bronze 5, 8, 16, 21, 24

chariots 20, 21, 28
cities 4, 7, 8, 9, 10, 14,
 20, 30
clay (and clay tablets)
 5, 13, 19, 24, 25, 26, 31
climate 4

clothes 29
communities 4, 5, 8, 12, 20
crafts/craftsmen 10, 24

domesticating 6, 7
droughts 12, 13

families 8, 11, 19
farming 5, 6, 7, 13, 18, 22,
 23, 26, 30
festivals 13, 14, 15
fishing 23
floods/floodplains 4, 5,
 12, 17
fortune tellers 20

gardens 11, 23
gods/goddesses 8, 9, 12, 13,
 14, 15, 16, 17, 20, 24,
 26, 27, 29, 31
gold 10, 24, 25, 30

hair 29
horoscopes 31
houses 10, 11
hunting 7, 10, 21, 23, 25

inventions 6, 18, 26, 30, 31
Iraq 4, 7, 11, 13, 15, 17,
 25, 29
irrigation 5, 22, 23

jewelery 24

kings 5, 8, 9, 10, 11, 18, 20,
 25, 30

landowners 9
laws/Law Code 9, 18, 19

magic 16, 27
makeup 29
mathematics 26, 31

medicine 27
music 13, 28-29
myths 11, 16, 17, 29

nomads 6, 7
palaces 8, 10, 11, 15, 20, 25
planets 27, 31
pottery 25
prayers 13
priests/priestesses 13, 14, 15,
 26, 27, 30, 31

reading 16, 19
rivers 4, 5, 16, 23
roads 30

scribes 19
sheep 7, 18, 23, 26
slaves 8, 9
society 5, 8, 10, 18
soldiers 20

songs 13, 29
stars 27, 31
statues 9, 12, 13, 15, 24, 25,
 28, 29
Sumer(ians) 4, 5, 20, 26

temples 13, 14, 15
time 31
towns 7, 8, 14, 15, 30

villages 4, 6, 7

wars/warfare 10, 20, 21
water 5, 20, 22
weapons 21
wheels 30
women 8, 9, 15, 17, 29
worshiping 12, 14, 15
writing 10, 18, 19, 26, 30

ziggurats 14, 15

TIME LINE OF MESOPOTAMIA

COMMUNITIES 9000-5000 B.C.

9000 B.C. *First animals and plants are domesticated from the wild.*

8000 B.C. *First known village is established in Jarmo.*

PRE-SUMERIANS 5000-3500 B.C.

5000 B.C. *First labor and first religious shrines.*

4700 B.C. *Pottery making is first practiced.*

3900 B.C. *First evidence of temples.*

SUMERIANS 3500-1900 B.C.

3500 B.C. *Sumerians settle near the Euphrates River. The Temple at Eridu is built.*

3000 B.C. *the pictograph and cuneiform writing systems are introduced. Wooden wheels are invented.*

2334-2150 B.C. *Sargon I begins the Akkadian rule.*

BABYLONIANS AND ASSYRIANS 1792-539 B.C.

1800-1170 B.C. *Old Babylonian period.*

1728-1685 B.C. *Hammurabi gains control of most of Mesopotamia. He introduces the Code of Laws.*

1600-1100 B.C. *Staggered periods of Hittite and Kassite rule over Mesopotamia.*

1200-612 B.C. *Assyrian period.*

714-681 B.C. *Reign of Sennacherib.*

668-626 B.C. *Reign of Ashurbanipal*

612 B.C. *Fall of Nineveh.*

612-539 B.C. *Neo-Babylonian Period*

630-562 B.C. *Reign of Nebuchadnezzar. Legend says he built the Hanging Gardens of Babylon.*

539 B.C. *Fall of Babylon.*